On The Job

at a Farm

by Jessica Cohn

RED
CHAIR
·PRESS·

Please visit our website at **www.redchairpress.com** for more high-quality products for young readers.

Publisher's Cataloging-In-Publication Data

Cohn, Jessica.
   On the job at a farm / by Jessica Cohn.

   pages : illustrations ; cm. -- (On the job)

   Summary: "Do you like helping people? Would you like to help feed hundreds of people each day? Then you might like to go On the Job at a Farm. Discover what the key business of farming is all about."--Provided by publisher.

   Includes writing activity and first-person interview.
   Includes bibliographical references and index.
   ISBN: 978-1-63440-112-8 (library hardcover)
   ISBN: 978-1-63440-118-0 (paperback)
   ISBN: 978-1-937529-81-9 (ebook)

   1. Agriculture--Vocational guidance--Juvenile literature. 2. Farmers--Juvenile literature. 3. Agriculture--Vocational guidance. 4. Farmers. I. Title. II. Title: At a farm

S519 .C64 2016
630.203   2015953633

Illustration credits: Illustration credits: p. 4, 5, 8, 12, 15, 16, 17, 18, 19, 22, 23, 26, 27, 28, 30: Lauren Scheuer

Photo credits: Cover, p. 1, 8, 9 (top), 16-17, 17, 20 (right), 21 (left, right), 28: Shutterstock; p. 3, 4, 5 (top, middle), 6-7, 7, 9 (bottom), 10, 10-11, 12 (bottom left, bottom), 14-15, 15, 18, 19 (bottom left, bottom right), 22 (middle left, middle right), 23 (top), 29: Dreamstime; p. 13, 20 (left), 22 (bottom), 23 (bottom), 26-27, 27: iStock; p. 24, 25: Lindsey Jahn, Food Research Institute; p. 32: Nathan Cohn

This series first published by:
Red Chair Press LLC   PO Box 333   South Egremont, MA 01258-0333

Printed in the United States of America

Distributed in the U.S. by Lerner Publisher Services. www.lernerbooks.com

0516 1 WRZF16

Table of Contents

Jobs in Agriculture

America is like a huge farmers market. New produce keeps coming into season. Each region has the right weather for certain fruits and vegetables.

The state fruit of Washington is the apple. That is because six out of ten apples come from there. Wisconsin grows the most cranberries. They grow well in the sandy and wet areas of the state.

Growers like Gil Schieber, of Washington, are busy all year long. His orchard has 1,600 trees. He says he is "busiest in spring." The branches of the apple trees need to be thinned. The workers have to get rid of weeds and insects. They need to build new structures, such as frames for the plants to grow on.

World Harvest

Agriculture is a giant business in America. One in three acres grows food that is sold to other countries. For example, U.S. farms grow half of all corn grown world-wide.

A lot of corn is made into ethanol, a fuel that burns more cleanly than oil. Many crops are raw materials that get used in other products. For example, cotton plants grow well on farms in the South. The cotton fibers can be made into cloth.

You Know It!

STEM stands for
Science, Technology,
Engineering, and Math.
These studies are
important in farming.
People are applying their skills
to the food supply. It needs
to be big enough to feed
a growing world.

Everybody's Business

Agriculture is the science and practice of farming. But planting crops is just the start of food production. The food must get from the farm to the refrigerator.

Food companies make raw foods into soups, snacks, and other goods. Pizza has been named the favorite food in America. It is a common treat. But a lot of work goes into each pizza. Someone raises tomatoes for the sauce. A farmer grows grains for the crust. Others raise cows and goats for milk. The milk is made into the cheese. A box company makes the box.

Granaries store wheat and other cereal grains.

Why will people always need food?

A person's body digests food, or breaks it into parts the body can use. Food is made of **molecules**. The molecules are made of atoms. Those are the basic units of living and nonliving things. There is energy in the connections between atoms. Digestion breaks the connections, and bodies take the energy from there.

Growing Fields

Agribusiness is the business tied to farming. Some people make and sell farm supplies. Some companies store the products that come from farms. Others take the products to markets. They are all part of this business as well.

Agriculture is the basis of many kinds of careers. About 1 percent of Americans work on farms. Another 22 million Americans work in jobs that have a connection to farming.

Family Farming

"This is an exciting time for farmers and ranchers of all types and sizes as agriculture is a bright spot in the American economy."
—Tom Vilsack, U.S. Secretary of Agriculture

Any area where crops or livestock grow is a farm. But a farm could be an orchard, with fruit trees. It could be a truck farm that grows flowers. One mom has a blog about her family's life on their farm. "Every day is different," she writes. She and her family have a hog farm.

Families or individuals own most U.S. farms. But their farms come in many sizes. Some family members may work at other jobs because their farms are too small to support them. But another individual may own thousands of acres of land and employ many hundreds of people.

Day Cares

One thing that farmers have in common is their unending work. There is an old joke. It starts with "Why do people look up to farmers?" It ends with "They are out standing in their fields," an answer that is also fitting. Each day, farmers set out to water their crops. They feed **nutrients** to their plants. Ranchers wake up early to care for the animals.

On Schieber's orchard, they have a nursery, where they grow new plants. In addition, growers must repair tools and machines. Farmers have to take care of their bills. They need to keep track of their products

Big, Little, and In-Between

The government groups most farms by the sales they make each year.

Small family farm
$249,999 or less

Large family farm
$250,000 to $499,000

Very large family farm
$500,000 or more

Nonfamily All others

Source: U.S.D.A. Economic Research Service

9

Way of Life

Science helps growers make the most of their land. For example, Schieber has learned to keep **habitats** for helpful insects. The orchard raises bees because they help the fruit grow by pollination. The bees also make honey the orchard can sell.

On farms there is an ongoing loss of soil from the land's surface. Rain, ice, and wind wear away the dirt. But during the last 30 years, farmers have cut these effects by half. They have protected their lands with **conservation tillage**. They leave some parts of their crops on the dirt. This works like a blanket to help hold it in place.

Dirt can also wear out from being planted so much. So, farmers practice **crop rotation** to help the soil. They allow fields to rest during some seasons. They plant crops that put nutrients back into the dirt. Soil science is important in farming.

Path for a Farmer

Want to help feed the world? Like working with natural sciences? Not afraid of getting dirty? Saying yes to these questions is one step to becoming a farmer.

» You Know It!

On average, one U.S. farmer produces food for 155 people.

Getting the Job

Skills
Need problem solving, business, and STEM skills (plant and animal sciences)

Duties
Manage growing conditions. Make business plans. Know health and safety rules. Use rules from the government. Follow trends in agriculture.

Education
1. **Associate's degree** or **bachelor's degree** recommended, including science and business classes

2. Work closely with people who know agriculture.

3. May study special subjects, such as aquaculture.

Growing Industry

"The variation of crops and food handling systems is fascinating."
—Sean Feder, director of inspectors in Santa Cruz, California

Scientists have found many ways to grow more food on less land. For example, they have learned what to add to dirt to make seeds grow faster. This growth in farming makes it possible to keep prices low on many foods. But it has also raised some questions about the food supply.

Chemicals help food grow. They also keep food from rotting. But these same chemicals can end up in the meals people eat. So, food scientists are looking for more healthful ways to raise food in plenty. The fastest growing part of agriculture is **organic** farming.

Checking It Out

At a grocery store, shoppers look at produce. They wonder. Does it look ripe? Is it ready? Now, more shoppers are also asking if the food is organic. To be organic, the plants must be raised with fewer chemicals. The farms have to follow special rules.

Laws cover food safety, and there are people who check that the laws are followed. These inspectors work for the U.S. government. They visit food producers. They try to make sure the foods will not cause illness. But a farm needs to pass special tests for its crops to be called organic.

An inspector may prepare for the day in a home office. Then, he or she may drive to a farm or a place that handles food. There, the inspector meets with the workers. He or she reviews their plans and their place of work.

Sean Feder makes sure foods are organic, and he enjoys the work. "You get to meet many different people," he says, "and you get to travel and see the region or beyond."

It can take more than a day to visit a large place. But a small farm may just take an hour or so. The inspector then makes a report. It can take several hours to finish a report.

Big Operations

Some people enjoy solving problems, and people like this are needed in agriculture. Many of today's challenges will be fixed with the tools made by problem solvers. Already, new tools can better measure chemicals for crops. This may lead to less need for the substances.

Many farms use more water than they really need. But new meters can better measure the water in soil. This can cut down on waste. Computers can show how to get the most work done in the least time. This can lead to less need for farm machines, which can dirty the air and soil with their exhaust. Some newer engines can even make "clean" exhaust.

›› You Know It!

Nations with less technology need to use more land to produce the same amount of food.

Green Food

Many changes are in store for the food supply. Experts are studying plants to find new uses for them. For example, some scientists are making electricity from plant parts.

A number of companies are creating new foods from plant life. Some plants are being raised to replace meat. Animals raised for meat need a great deal of food and water. Greenery needs less time and attention. So, this effort may help the **environment**.

Scientists study plant and soil samples in bio labs.

What is sustainable farming?

People who farm this way want to protect the environment. They try to cut waste. These farmers consider the effects of chemicals. They look for safe and healthful ways to operate.

Living Science

Raising livestock is a big part of agriculture. In fact, beef production is the biggest part of U.S. agriculture. In the old days, most of the cattle grew on ranches. Ranchers rode horses to do their work. They drove their cattle to market by herding the animals along. Today, most meat and **poultry** come from large feedlots.

Factory farms are large lots where animals are kept close together. This can breed sickness. The medicines to keep the animals well can end up in their meat. So, people keep looking for better ways to raise them.

Jobs with Animals

New tools can gather important information about the animals. For example, new tracking tools allow some animals to walk around more. There is less need for some of the medicines.

Some ranchers can let their animals roam and use helicopters to watch them. Cows now have collars that track their diets. Tools can also show how much milk cows are making.

This area of agriculture needs people with new ideas, too. Many jobs have to do with raising animals. The work includes the following:

- Range manager
- Animal **physiologist**
- **Nutritionist**
- **Ecology** manager

What is fish and wildlife management?

Some people work with fish and other animals in their natural homes, such as lakes and forests. Their work is often tied to agriculture. For example, some people help farmers by getting rid of pests.

> ## >> You Know It!
>
> Diets are part of animal science. The food that animals eat ends up in their meat. Animals raised on regular grass make meat that differs from those that eat feed made in factories.

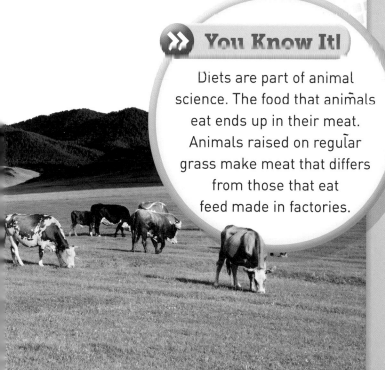

By the Numbers

"I love working with people and problem solving."
—Reb Botelho, transportation manager for a fruit company in Watsonville, California

Growing crops and raising animals is the heart of food production. But the industry offers many other kinds of jobs, such as in **packaging**. Many people work in **processing**. People also have jobs moving food from one place to another.

Workers in the **supply chain** figure out how to move products. They find the smartest ways to send raw foods to companies that use them. They decide how food will go to markets.

"I have worked in the supply chain since I was 21," says Reb Botelho. "As a kid I was very organized."

To Market

Botelho went to school to learn to do the work. The classes included **inventory** management. Botelho learned better ways of planning. Supplies must be picked up at certain times. Products must be delivered when they are expected. It is a large puzzle to work out. It includes many people and places.

"It's fun to improve areas that are [a mess]," says Botelho. "I also loved to play team sports as a kid, so being on a team working in a group also made supply chain a natural fit for me."

Miles of Food
The average U.S. meal includes food that has traveled **1,500 miles**.

A head of lettuce often travels **more than 2,000 miles** to get to a table.

Supporting Roles in Farming

Many people support food production through the work they do. These include the many people who work at colleges, conducting studies and teaching others. STEM skills are needed for almost all jobs in farming.

Teachers and Professors

Research in agriculture goes on at colleges around the country. Professors teach people about this field. Some of the professors are experts in life sciences. Others know about the business of raising food or managing the land.

Veterinarians

These doctors are often called vets. They treat the diseases and injuries of animals. Vets also work to prevent sickness. They tend to work on either large animals, small animals, or animals that are thought of as unusual, or exotic. Vets who work on farms studied livestock when taking classes in college.

Geneticists

Seeds and other living things come with codes called **DNA**. These codes carry the features of each kind of plant or animal. The codes are made of smaller units called genes. Geneticists study them. These scientists work to grow stronger plants and animals.

Economists

Economics is the study of goods and services and how they are traded. Economists look at facts and figures. Some economists have a special interest in food. They help officials, farmers, and other businesspeople make decisions about the food supply.

Part of the Process

Two tomatoes were walking down the street. One was in front of the other. "Hey, ketchup!" it said to its pal.

Raw food such as tomatoes can be changed into other forms, like ketchup. Companies that do this are food processors. Most often, they make foods that are easy to prepare and to eat. These businesses often make items that last longer than raw food.

The top ten companies that do this include drink makers. The list includes companies that make cereal and pasta. Businesses that sell meat and poultry are part of the top ten, too.

Tomatoes on the production line getting washed.

Ready to Eat

Lasting longer is one benefit of processed foods. These foods can be carried long distances. Most people do not live near farms. So, this makes it is easier for everyone to eat a variety of meals. Some prepared foods even help some people stay healthy. For example, some people cannot eat sugar. It makes them sick, so they need special foods.

Prepared foods often cost less, which is another benefit. However, foods can lose nutrients when they are changed into another form. Some of the chemicals that help them last longer are not healthful. Many people are working to make these foods better for the people who eat them.

What can be improved in prepared foods?
People in food companies must consider how clean the food is kept. They think about the energy needed to make their products. These workers need to cut out waste. They want to improve the taste and healthfulness of their foods.

Talking to a Food Scientist

Adam Borger is a microbiologist at the University of Wisconsin-Madison. Micro means "tiny." Bio means "life." He studies microbes, which are tiny life forms. He says they come in three types: "the good, the bad, and the ugly." For example, some **bacteria** help people digest their food. But others can make people sick.

1 **How does someone become a food scientist?**

I got into this field . . . because I like to cook, and I like to do research on how to make food better.

I have two college degrees (bachelor's and **master's**). After college, I worked for two food companies as a microbiologist for 15 years before returning to a university to work.

2 **What is your day like?**

On a typical day I help different food companies answer questions about harmful microbes that are in foods and how to keep them out, kill them, or keep them from growing in the foods. I also teach people about microbiology.

3 What is the best part?

I like talking to students and adults. . . . That is my favorite part of the job. I get to travel around the country sometimes to talk to people and help them with questions.

Sometimes, people like Borger use a microscope to look at microbes. More often, they will grow a community of microbes. Then, they will test the small living things with tools that read DNA. If they find the DNA of a harmful microbe, they go after it.

On the Table

Farming is one of the oldest ways to make a living. But new opportunities tied to it are not running out any time soon. The food supply is key to the future. It is important for food scientists to keep the supply of foods healthful.

Farm tools are changing fast, and workers are needed to run and fix the new machines. Special robots are being made for fieldwork. The robots can pull weeds, shake fruit from trees, and even herd cattle. Most of the machines do the hard jobs that wear people out.

Changing Fast

Some people say that the robots will be normal on most farms by 2050. Other people say that it will take longer. Already, many large farms have tractors that drive themselves. The machines link to **satellites** that send messages from one place to another.

Farming is one of the oldest businesses on Earth. But it is going through fast changes now. Computers, robots, and **drones** are finding their way to the fields. People with STEM skills are needed in this industry.

Who is making robots for farms?

Teams at universities are working on new robots. They compete to win contests with their ideas. For example, a team at Kansas State University recently made a small machine on four wheels. It can drop a grain into the dirt every inch or so.

 You Know It!

Robots and other large automated machines can do the work of 20 or more people in fields and greenhouses. This can save farmers time and money.

Growing Heart

One seed company has a Web site where farmers post reasons why they farm. "Farming is a front row seat to miracles," says one. "It's more than a job. It's a way of life," says another. "You get to be part of history and the future," someone else posted.

Farming can be rewarding. But no one says it is an easy way of life. Buying land is costly. Paying taxes and renting land are, too. Keeping up with rules for farming can be difficult. A farmer may have all the newest tools, and weather can still ruin the crops.

At Work on a Farm

Grapes. Peaches. Beans. Corn. Wheat. Tomatoes. Seaweed. What would you want to grow?

Even crops are changing, so farmers need to keep up with the changes. For example, some farmers are raising seaweed for new uses. In fact, one of the areas for growth in farming is the sea. Already, people raise fish and shellfish. Now, scientists are working on ways to use seawater to raise crops. In one plan, seawater would be run through channels into the land. The waste that comes from each plant or animal would be used to help raise others.

Are you interested in the science of food?

Do you like to solve problems?

Can you see yourself getting and giving the training to manage food sources?

Perhaps you will one day work at a job . . . tied to farming.

Extension
Test It!

Scientists follow steps to test their ideas. Is there something about growing plants or animals that you would like to understand better? Why not check it out?

Before

Come up with the question you want answered. Think of a way to test for the answer. Then, make your best guess of how the test will turn out.

Experiments are all about causes and effects. So, think of a test that shows what leads to something else. Think of different factors or conditions that you can test and compare.

During

The best things to test are things that can be measured. At the very least, they should be things you can observe. Test each factor. Carefully record the results.

After

Review the results. Did they prove your best guess to be right? If not, that is normal. Science is all about testing for what is right, not just being right.

Write a report that describes your test. Explain your conclusions. Many times, your conclusions will include an idea for yet another experiment!

Glossary

associate's degree earned for one or two years of study after high school

bachelor's degree earned for three to five years of study after high school

bacteria group of one-cell life forms that live in, on, or away from other living things

chemicals substances that bond and change in certain ways when they interact

conservation tillage practices that save soil and its resources, such as water

crop rotation practice of planting crops in a certain order and at certain times to keep soil from wearing out

degrees notices awarded to people for advanced study

DNA materials inside cells that carry information about the features of living things and their growth

drones aircraft that do not carry people

ecology science of how living things relate to their surroundings

engineering science concerned with building or using machines and structures

environment surroundings or conditions

habitats natural environments of living things

inventory complete list of items

master's degree earned for mastery of subject at least one year beyond bachelor's degree

molecules smallest units of atoms that feature the properties of a given chemical

nutrients food parts that deliver substances needed to survive and grow

nutritionist someone who studies nutrients in food and their effects

organic adjective for food grown in a way that protects Earth; can mean food has passed tests that show it does not have certain chemicals

packaging covering for and protecting of products

physiologist someone who studies health in animal or plant tissues

poultry birds raised for meat, eggs, or feathers

processing in agriculture, the change of raw food to other forms

satellites objects placed into space to circle Earth, often acting as communication tools

supply chain system of or channel for moving items from their makers to other people

technology science applied to life and industry

Index

>> Meet the Author

Jessica Cohn has made a career of writing and editing materials for young people, covering varied topics, from social studies and science to poetry. If you ask her, Cohn will tell you that she feels lucky to be on the job in educational publishing. Each day, she discovers something new to learn and someone with an interesting story—and then gets to share the information. Jessica and her family reside in California. When not working, she enjoys hiking, helping her local library, and exploring the country.